Top FIFA Men's World Cup Finals

By Ryan James

A Stingray Book

SEAHORSE PUBLISHING

Teaching Tips for Caregivers and Teachers:

This Hi-Lo book features high-interest subject matter that will appeal to all readers in intermediate and middle school grades. It may be enjoyed by students reading at or above grade level as well as by those who are looking for age-appropriate themes matched with a less challenging reading level. Hi-Lo books are ideal for ELL readers, too.

Each book appeals to a striving reader's age and maturity level. Opportunities are provided for students to read words they already know while encountering a limited number of new, high-interest vocabulary words. With these supports in place, students will read more fluently while increasing reading comprehension. Use the following suggestions to help students grow as readers.

- Encourage the student to read independently at home.
- Encourage the student to practice reading aloud.
- Encourage activities that require reading.
- Establish a regular reading time.
- Have the student write questions about what they read.

Teaching Tips for Teachers:

Before Reading

- Ask, "What do I know about this topic?"
- Ask, "What do I want to learn about this topic?"

During Reading

- Ask, "What is the author trying to teach me?"
- Ask, "How is this like something I already know?"

After Reading

- Discuss how the text features (headings, index, etc.) help with understanding the topic.
- Ask, "What interesting or fun fact did you learn?"

TABLE OF CONTENTS

What Is the FIFA Men's World Cup Final?

The FIFA (Fédération Internationale de Football Association) Men's World Cup is an **international** soccer tournament played every four years between 32 different teams. The final game decides which country has the best men's soccer team in the world.

The first World Cup Final took place on July 30, 1930, when Uruguay won 4 to 2 against Argentina.

Currently, teams must **qualify** during the three years before each tournament.

FUN FACT: A dog named Pickles found a stolen FIFA Men's World Cup trophy. He received a lifetime supply of dog food.

2018 FIFA Men's World Cup Final

July 15, 2018

FRANCE 4 - 2 CROATIA

LUZHNIKI STADIUM, MOSCOW, RUSSIA

A Croatian player tried to head the ball away from the goal, but it went past the goalkeeper instead. This was the first-ever **own goal** in a FIFA Men's World Cup Final.

Teenager Kylian Mbappé from France made a shot from 25 yards (23 meters).

Mario Mandžukić from Croatia kicked a loose ball into an unguarded net.

The match finished with a Men's World Cup high score.

GOLDEN BALL AWARD:
LUKA MODRIĆ

1974 FIFA Men's World Cup Final

July 7, 1974

WEST GERMANY 2 - 1 NETHERLANDS

OLYMPIASTADION, MUNICH, GERMANY

The Netherlands scored in the first two minutes starting from a penalty kick.

In the 25th minute, West Germany scored on a second penalty kick to tie the match.

This was the first time these penalty kicks happened in a FIFA Men's World Cup Final.

Late in the first half, soccer great Gerd Müller of West Germany scored the final goal. Müller retired after the game.

GOLDEN BALL AWARD:

JOHAN CRUYFF

2006 FIFA Men's World Cup Final

July 9, 2006

ITALY **5-3** (penalty kicks) FRANCE

OLYMPIASTADION, BERLIN, GERMANY

At minute 104, Italian goalkeeper Gianluigi Buffon blocked a **header** from star French player Zinédine Zidane.

Minutes later, Italian Marco Materazzi tugged on Zidane's jersey. Officials did not see it happen.

Zidane headbutted Materazzi's chest and knocked him to the ground. Zidane got a **red card**.

The match was tied 1 to 1. It went to a penalty shoot-out without Zidane. Italian Fabio Grosso scored the winning penalty kick.

GOLDEN BALL AWARD:
ZINÉDINE ZIDANE

2010 FIFA Men's World Cup Final

July 11, 2010

SPAIN 1-0 NETHERLANDS

SOCCER CITY, JOHANNESBURG, SOUTH AFRICA

This was a physical match with many penalties. There were 14 **yellow cards** and one red card.

There were few attempts on goal. One opportunity came when Dutch player Arjen Robben went one-on-one with Spanish goalkeeper Iker Casillas. Casillas intercepted Robben's shot with the toe of his shoe.

At the end of 90 minutes, neither team had scored. The game went into extra time.

Cesc Fàbregas passed the ball to Andrés Iniesta, who scored the game-winning goal for Spain.

GOLDEN BALL AWARD:
DIEGO FORLÁN

2014 FIFA Men's World Cup Final

July 13, 2014

GERMANY 1-0 ARGENTINA

MARACANÃ STADIUM, RIO DE JANEIRO, BRAZIL

Forward Thomas Müller and goalkeeper Manuel Neuer led Germany. Argentina was led by forwards Lionel Messi and Gonzalo Higuaín.

Defender Benedikt Höwedes headed the ball toward Germany's goal. This gave Argentina's Gonzalo Higuaín an easy shot. However, he missed.

The score was 0 to 0 after 90 minutes. The match went into extra time.

In minute 113, German Mario Götze controlled the ball on his chest. He kicked it into the net to score the match's only goal.

GOLDEN BALL AWARD:
LIONEL MESSI

1998 FIFA Men's World Cup Final

July 12, 1998

FRANCE 3-0 BRAZIL

STADE DE FRANCE, SAINT-DENIS, FRANCE

Brazil was favored heavily to win.

Hours before the match, star Brazilian player Ronaldo lost consciousness and was in the hospital.

He recovered and was able to play.

Brazil had six shots on goal, but they were all blocked by goalkeeper Fabien Barthez.

At the end of the match, Emmanuel Petit kicked the ball low into the net to earn France its first World Cup title.

GOLDEN BALL AWARD:
RONALDO

1990 FIFA Men's World Cup Final

July 8, 1990

WEST GERMANY 1-0 ARGENTINA

STADIO OLIMPICO, ROME, ITALY

West Germany was led by forwards Rudi Völler and Jürgen Klinsmann. Argentina was led by midfielders Diego Maradona and Jorge Burruchaga.

Argentina's Roberto Sensini **fouled** Rudi Völler. This gave a penalty kick to West Germany and allowed Andreas Brehme to score the match's only goal.

West German coach and former team captain Franz Beckenbauer became the first person to both captain and coach a winning Men's World Cup team.

GOLDEN BALL AWARD:

SALVATORE SCHILLACI

1994 FIFA Men's World Cup Final

July 17, 1994

BRAZIL	3 - 2 (penalty kicks)	ITALY

ROSE BOWL, PASADENA, CALIFORNIA, UNITED STATES

At the end of **regulation** play, neither team had scored. Penalty kicks would decide the winner in a shoot-out.

Brazilian captain Dunga scored a match point.

It was up to Italian Roberto Baggio to keep his team's dream alive. He kicked the ball over the bar.

Brazil won their fourth Men's World Cup title.

GOLDEN BALL AWARD:
ROMÁRIO DE SOUZA FARIA

GLOSSARY

fouled (fowld): had a player violate the rules against you

header (HED-ur): a shot or pass in soccer made by hitting the ball with your head

international (in-tur-NASH-uh-nuhl): involving more than one country

own goal (ohn gohl): a goal that a player accidentally scores against their own team

qualify (KWAH-luh-fye): to reach a standard or level that allows you to do something

red card (red kahrd): a red card that a referee holds in the air to show that a player who has broken the rules will not be allowed to continue playing

regulation (reg-yuh-LAY-shuhn): the normal length of the time of play in a game

yellow cards (YEL-oh kahrdz): yellow cards that a referee holds in the air to give an official warning to a player who has broken the rules

INDEX

AFTER READING QUESTIONS

1. Which teams played in the 2018 Men's World Cup Final?
2. Which matches had goals from penalty kicks?
3. How often is the FIFA Men's World Cup played?
4. Explain Ronaldo's role in the 1998 Men's World Cup Final.
5. What is the difference between a yellow card and a red card?

About the Author

Ryan James lives in the western part of North Carolina with his dog Bailey. As a young child, his favorite soccer player was Lionel Messi and team FC Barcelona. When he's not watching soccer games, he goes hiking and biking in the mountains near his home.

Written by: Ryan James
Cover Design by: Rhea Magaro-Wallace
Interior Design by: Kathy Walsh
Editor: Kim Thompson

Library of Congress PCN Data
Top FIFA Men's World Cup Finals / Ryan James
Top Sports Championships
ISBN 978-1-63897-486-4 (hard cover)
ISBN 978-1-63897-601-1 (paperback)
ISBN 978-1-63897-716-2 (EPUB)
ISBN 978-1-63897-831-2 (eBook)
Library of Congress Control Number: 2022933969

Printed in the United States of America.

Photographs/Shutterstock: Cover ©winui, ©Kyodo/Newscom; Title Pg ©winui, ©EFKS; Pg 3 ©EFKS; Pg 4, 6, 8, 10, 12, 14, 16, 18, 20 ©Sedulur Grafis; Pg 7, 9, 11, 13, 15, 17, 19, 21 ©Little_Monster_2070, ©gualtiero boffi; Pg 5 ©Represented by ZUMA Press, Inc.; Pg 6 ©Kyodo/Newscom; Pg 8 ©@Wiki; Pg 10 ©THIERRY GROMIK; Pg 12 ©Andrew Boyers; Pg 14 ©Represented by ZUMA Press, Inc.; Pg 16 ©Bongarts/SportsChrome; Pg 18 ©JuhaTamminen; Pg 20 ©Icon Sports Media, Inc.

Seahorse Publishing Company
www.seahorsepub.com

Published in the United States
Seahorse Publishing
PO Box 771325
Coral Springs, FL 33077

SEAHORSE PUBLISHING